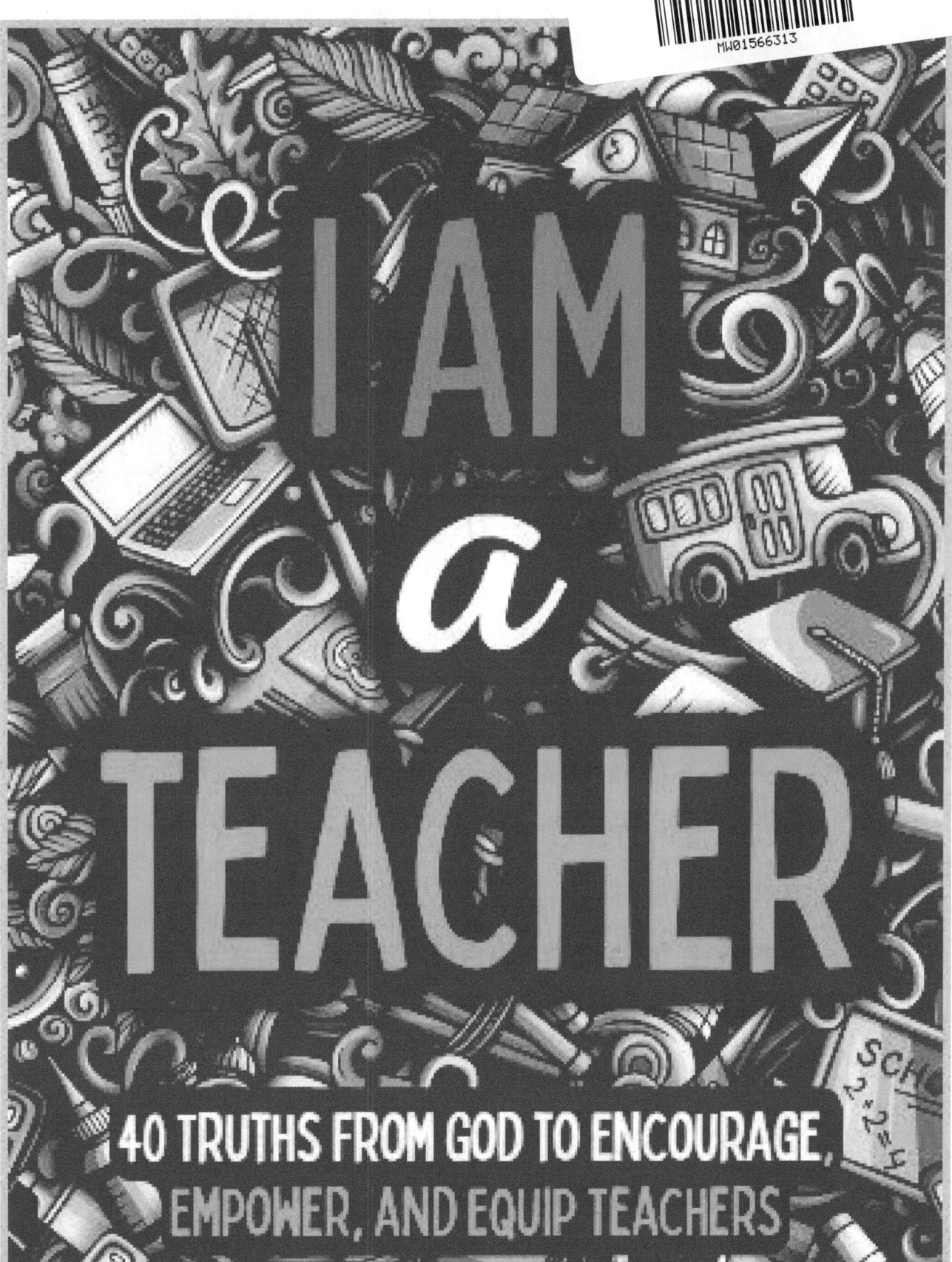

©2022 by Michelle Post, Ph.D.

All rights reserved. No portion of this book may be reproduced, stored in a retrieval system, or transmitted in
any form or by any means—electronic, mechanical, photocopy, recording, scanning, or other—except for brief quotations in critical reviews or articles, without the prior written permission of the author.

Published by The Tree of Love, LLC
https://thetreeoflove.org/

Printed in the United States of America

Front Matter and Back Matter
by Michelle Post, Ph.D.

Book Cover & Coloring Pages
by Digitalworld25

I am a Teacher

Show yourself in all respects to be a model of good works, and in your teaching show integrity, dignity, and sound speech that cannot be condemned, so that an opponent may be put to shame, having nothing evil to say about us.
Titus 2:7-8 ESV

Prayer of Encouragement

Heavenly Father, thank You for the teacher reading this prayer. I ask that You will protect them, encourage them, and hold them. Remind them daily that they are Your beloved child. Equip and empower them as they educate and encourage their students. Give them strength to continue on, knowing that their work is not in vain. Surround them with your hedge of protection, that they may teach with joy and peace of mind. In Jesus name, Amen.

The Truths of Who God Is
...Just a Few

- **God is Love** - The one who does not love does not know God, for God is love. 1 John 4:8 NASB
- **God is Truth** - For His lovingkindness is great toward us, and the truth of the Lord is everlasting. Praise the Lord! Psalm 117:2 NASB
- **God is Good** - For You, Lord, are good, and ready to forgive, and abundant in lovingkindness to all who call upon You. Psalm 86:5 NASB
- **God is Trustworthy** - . . . so that by two unchangeable things in which it is impossible for God to lie, we who have taken refuge would have strong encouragement to take hold of the hope set before us. Hebrews 6:18 NASB
- **God is Forgiving** - For you, O Lord, are good and forgiving, abounding in steadfast love to all who call upon you. Psalm 86:5 ESV
- **God is Just** - The Rock, his work is perfect, for all his ways are justice. A God of faithfulness and without iniquity, just and upright is He. Deuteronomy 32:4 ESV
- **God is Everywhere** - In the beginning was the Word, and the Word was with God, and the Word was God. He was in the beginning with God. All things were made through him, and without him was not any thing made that was made. In him was life,[a] and the life was the light of men. The light shines in the darkness, and the darkness has not overcome it. John 1:1-5 ESV
- **God is Faithful** - Know therefore that the LORD your God is God; he is the faithful God, keeping his covenant of love to a thousand generations of those who love him and keep his commandments. Deuteronomy 7:9 NIV
- **God is Gracious** - Gracious is the Lord, and righteous; yes, our God is compassionate. Psalm 116:5 NASB
- **God is Merciful** - Then the Lord passed by in front of him and proclaimed, "The Lord, the Lord God, compassionate and gracious, slow to anger, and abounding in lovingkindness and truth . . . Exodus 34:6 NASB
- **God is Constant** - Every good thing given and every perfect gift is from above, coming down from the Father of lights, with whom there is no variation or shifting shadow. James 1:17 NASB
- **God is All-Knowing** - For the word of God is living and active, sharper than any two-edged sword, piercing to the division of soul and of spirit, of joints and of marrow, and discerning the thoughts and intentions of the heart. And no creature is hidden from his sight, but all are naked and exposed to the eyes of him to whom we must give account. Hebrews 4:12-13 ESV

I am a Teacher

Show yourself in all respects to be a model of good works, and in your teaching show integrity, dignity, and sound speech that cannot be condemned, so that an opponent may be put to shame, having nothing evil to say about us.
Titus 2:7-8 ESV

I am an Influencer

. . . let your light shine before others, that they may see your good deeds and glorify your Father in heaven.
Matthew 5:16b NIV

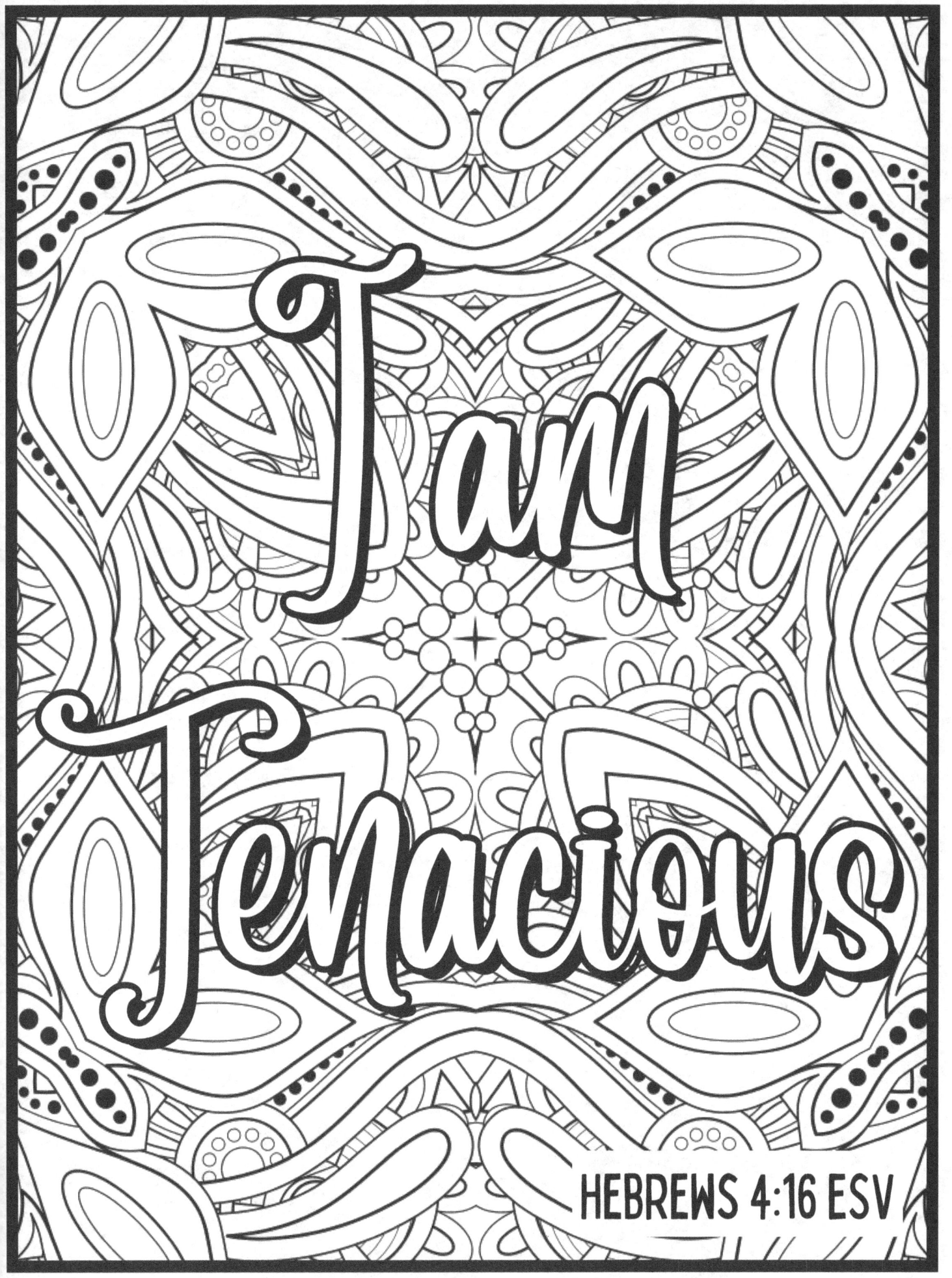

I am Tenacious

Let us then with confidence draw near to the throne of grace, that we may receive mercy and find grace to help in time of need.
Hebrews 4:16 ESV

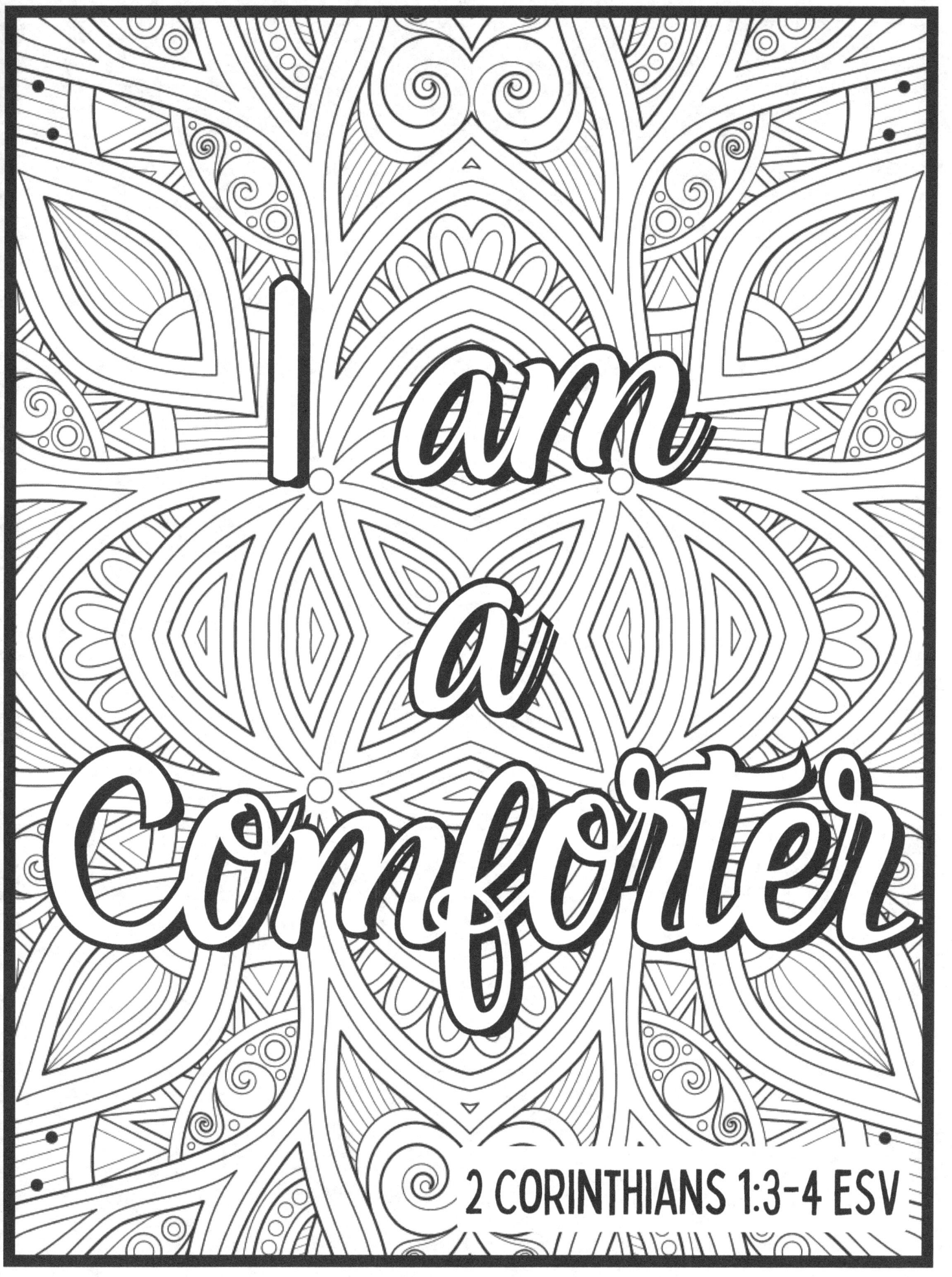

I am a Comforter

Blessed be the God and Father of our Lord Jesus Christ, the Father of mercies and God of all comfort, who comforts us in all our affliction, so that we may be able to comfort those who are in any affliction, with the comfort with which we ourselves are comforted by God.
2 Corinthians 1:3-4 ESV

I am Mindful

And do not be conformed to this world, but be transformed by the renewing of your mind, that you may prove what is that good and acceptable and perfect will of God.
Romans 12:2 NKJV

I am a Helper

Two are better than one, because they have a good reward for their toil. For if they fall, one will lift up his fellow. But woe to him who is alone when he falls and has not another to lift him up!
Ecclesiastes 4:9-10 ESV

I am Capable

I can do all things through Christ who strengthens me.
Philippians 4:13 NKJV

I am Decisive

But let your 'Yes' be 'Yes,' and your 'No,' 'No.' For whatever is more than these is from the evil one.
Matthew 5:37 NKJV

I am a Sharpener

Iron sharpens iron, and one man sharpens another.
Proverbs 27:17 ESV

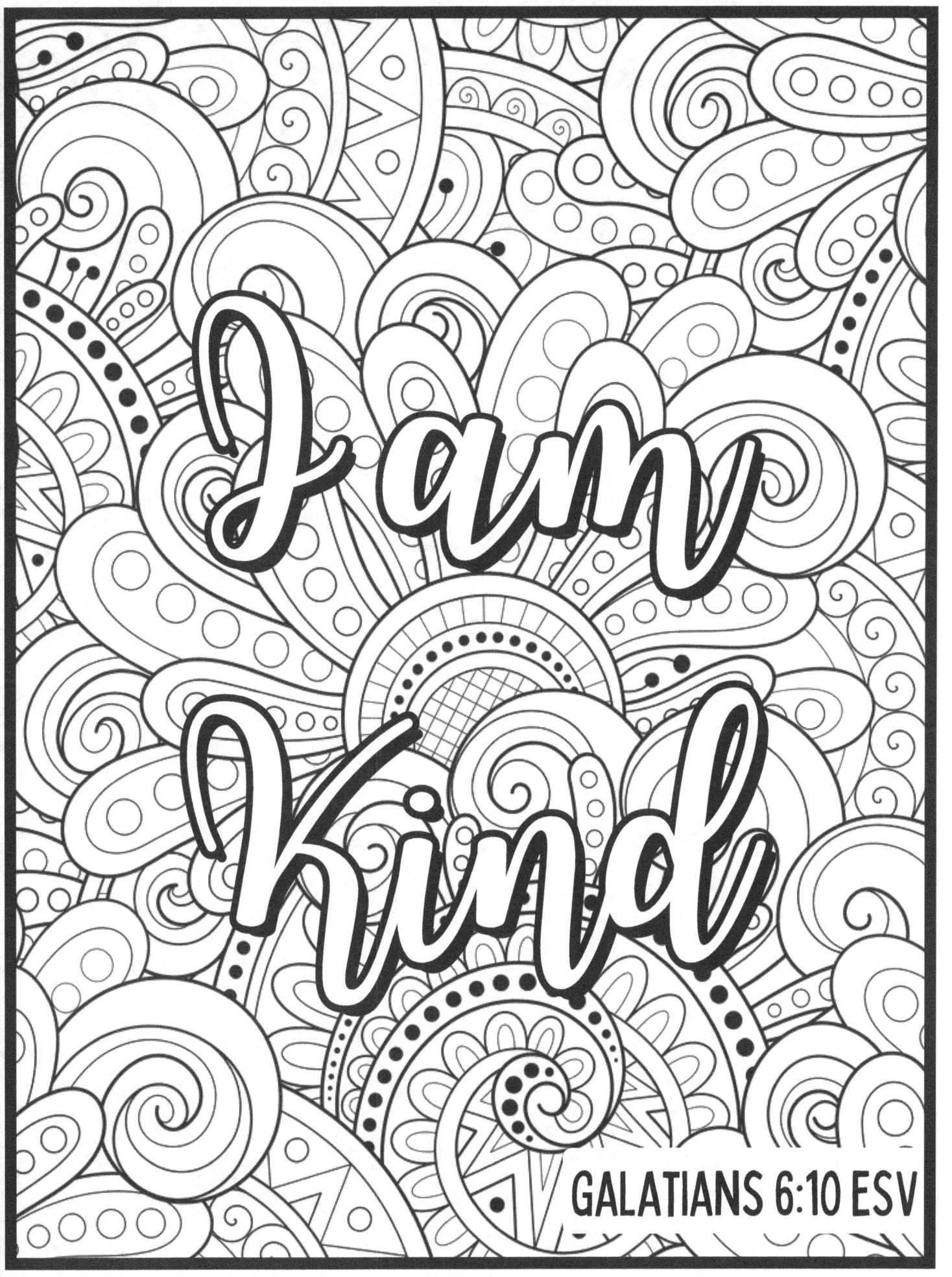

I am Kind

So then, as we have opportunity, let us do good to everyone, and especially to those who are of the household of faith.
Galatians 6:10 ESV

I am Adaptable

Not that I speak in regard to need, for I have learned in whatever state I am, to be content.
Philippians 4:11 NKJV

I am an Encourager

Therefore encourage one another and build one another up, just as you are doing.
1 Thessalonians 5:11 ESV

I am Listening

Consequently, faith comes from hearing the message, and the message is heard through the word about Christ.
Romans 10:17 NIV

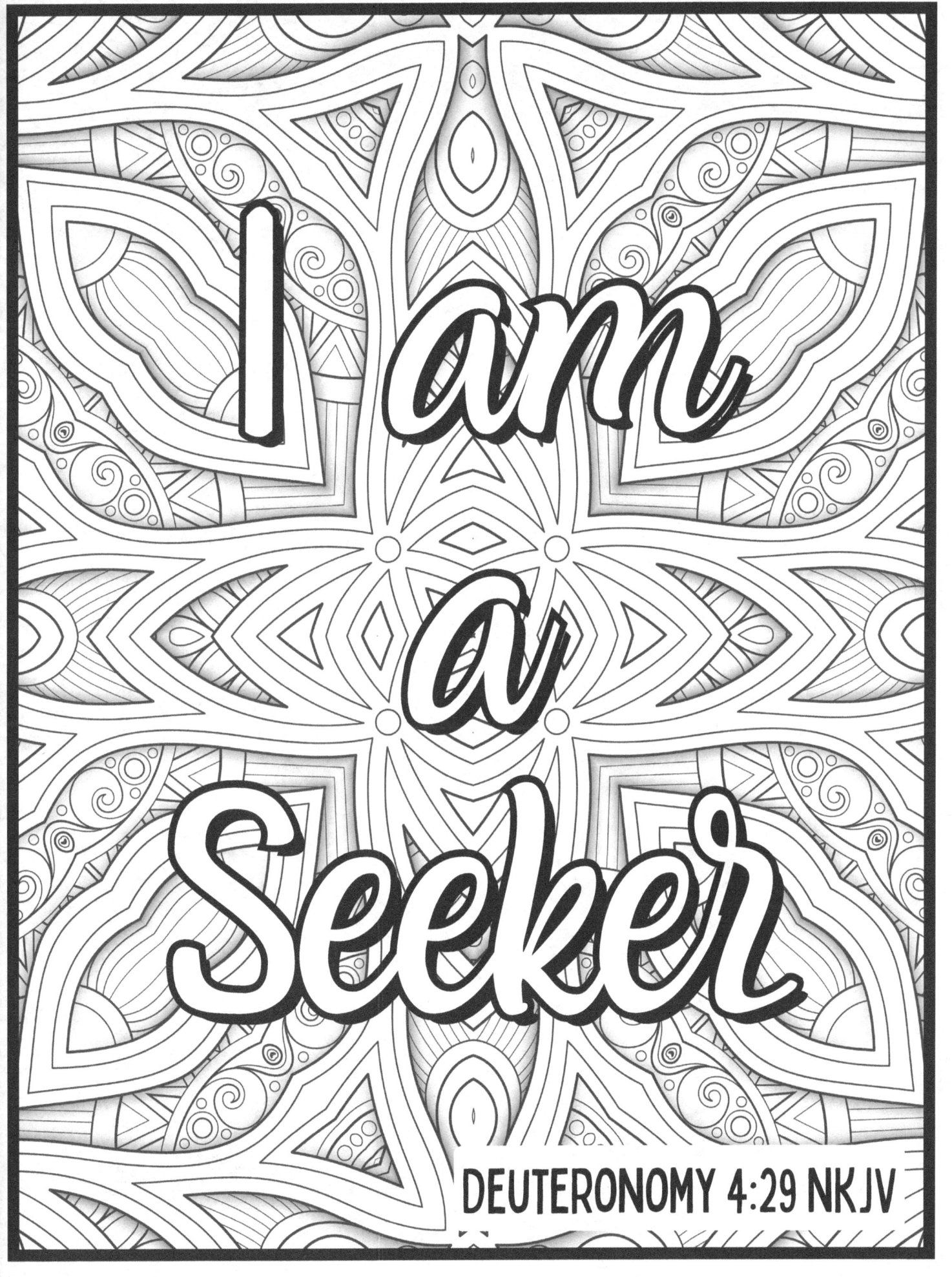

I am a Seeker

But from there you will seek the Lord your God, and you will find Him if you seek Him with all your heart and with all your soul.
Deuteronomy 4:29 NKJV

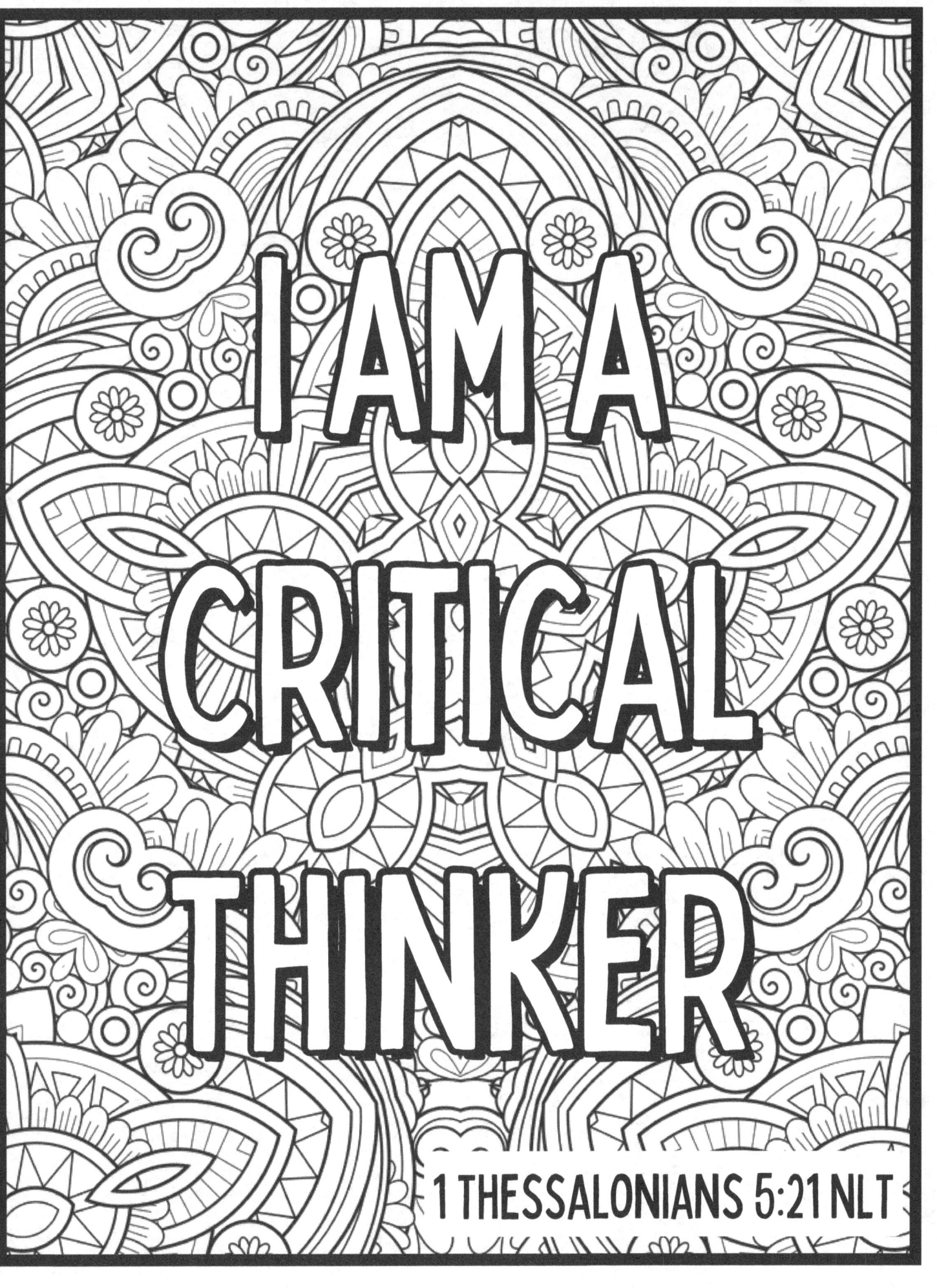

I am a Critical Thinker

But test everything that is said.
Hold on to what is good.
1 Thessalonians 5:21 NLT

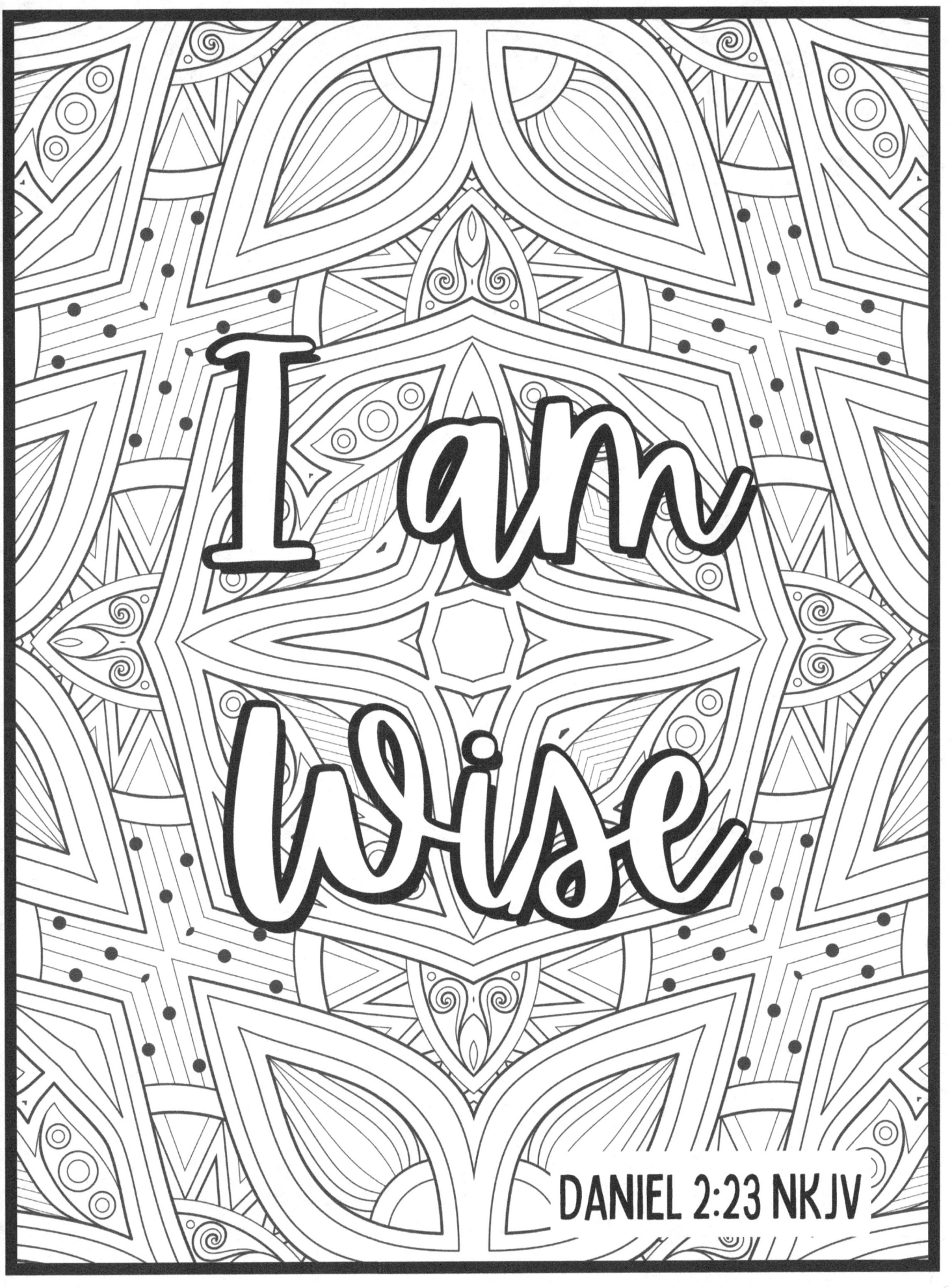

I am Wise

"I thank You and praise You, O God of my fathers; You have given me wisdom and might, and have now made known to me what we asked of You, for You have made known to us the king's demand."
Daniel 2:23 NKJV

I am Competent

That the man of God may be competent, equipped for every good work.
2 Timothy 3:17 ESV

I am Giving

Give, and it will be given to you. Good measure, pressed down, shaken together, running over, will be put into your lap. For with the measure you use it will be measured back to you.
Luke 6:38 ESV

I am Educated

As for you, the anointing you received from him remains in you, and you do not need anyone to teach you. But as his anointing teaches you about all things and as that anointing is real, not counterfeit—just as it has taught you, remain in him.
1 John 2:27 NIV

I am Empowered

And we know that the Son of God has come, and he has given us understanding so that we can know the true God. And now we live in fellowship with the true God because we live in fellowship with his Son, Jesus Christ. He is the only true God, and he is eternal life.
1 John 5:20 NLT

I am Diligent

The soul of the sluggard craves and gets nothing, while the soul of the diligent is richly supplied.
Proverbs 13:4 ESV

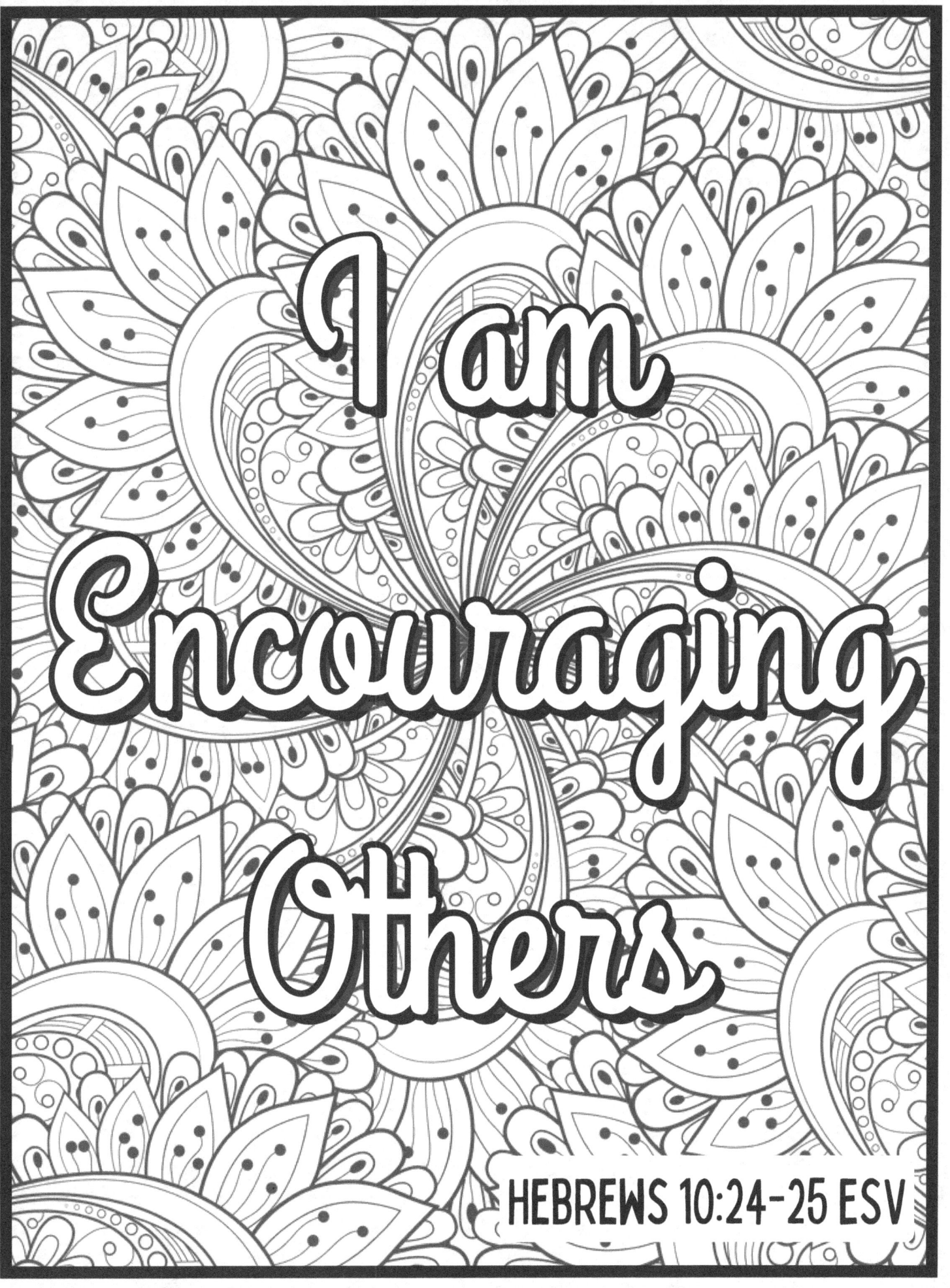

I am Encouraging Others

And let us consider how to stir up one another to love and good works, not neglecting to meet together, as is the habit of some, but encouraging one another, and all the more as you see the Day drawing near.
Hebrews 10:24-25 ESV

I am Respectful

Don't forget to show hospitality to strangers, for some who have done this have entertained angels without realizing it!
Hebrews 13:2 NLT

I am a Leader

Let love be genuine. Abhor what is evil; hold fast to what is good. Love one another with brotherly affection. Outdo one another in showing honor. Do not be slothful in zeal, be fervent in spirit, serve the Lord. Rejoice in hope, be patient in tribulation, be constant in prayer. Contribute to the needs of the saints and seek to show hospitality.
Romans 12:9-13 ESV

I am Enthusiastic

Always work enthusiastically for the Lord, for you know that nothing you do for the Lord is ever useless.
1 Corinthians 15:58b NLT

I am Able

Don't be afraid, for I am with you. Don't be discouraged, for I am your God. I will strengthen you and help you. I will hold you up with my victorious right hand.
Isaiah 41:10 NLT

I am Focused

Redeeming the time, because the days are evil.
Ephesians 5:16 NKJV

I am Thoughtful

He has showered his kindness on us, along with all wisdom and understanding.
Ephesians 1:8 NLT

I am Compassionate

You must be compassionate, just as your Father is compassionate.
Luke 6:36 NLT

I am Bold

The wicked run away when no one is chasing them, but the godly are as bold as lions.
Proverbs 28:1 NLT

I am Knowledgeable

Asking God, the glorious Father of our Lord Jesus Christ, to give you spiritual wisdom and insight so that you might grow in your knowledge of God.
Ephesians 1:17 NLT

I am a Learner

I will instruct you and teach you in the way you should go; I will counsel you with my loving eye on you.
Psalm 32:8 NIV

I am Confident

Therefore do not cast away your confidence, which has great reward.
Hebrews 10:35 NKJV

I am Qualified

And giving joyful thanks to the Father, who has qualified you to share in the inheritance of his holy people in the kingdom of light.
Colossians 1:12 NIV

I am Valuable

Look at the birds. They don't plant or harvest or store food in barns, for your heavenly Father feeds them. And aren't you far more valuable to him than they are?
Matthew 6:26 NLT

I am Productive

Yes, I am the vine; you are the branches. Those who remain in me, and I in them, will produce much fruit. For apart from me you can do nothing.
John 15:5 NLT

I am Resilient

Do not gloat over me, my enemies! For though I fall, I will rise again. Though I sit in darkness, the Lord will be my light.
Micah 7:8 NLT

I am Serving Others

Their responsibility is to equip God's people to do his work and build up the church, the body of Christ.
Ephesians 4:12 NLT

I am Trying

Not that I have already obtained all this, or have already arrived at my goal, but I press on to take hold of that for which Christ Jesus took hold of me.
Philippians 3:12 NIV

I am Unstoppable

. . . for though the righteous fall seven times, they rise again, but the wicked stumble when calamity strikes.
Proverbs 24:16 NIV

The Tree of Love, LLC
Sharing Who God Says You Are

- **I am a Teacher** - Show yourself in all respects to be a model of good works, and in your teaching show integrity, dignity, and sound speech that cannot be condemned, so that an opponent may be put to shame, having nothing evil to say about us. Titus 2:7-8 ESV
- **I am an Influencer** - . . . let your light shine before others, that they may see your good deeds and glorify your Father in heaven. Matthew 5:16b NIV
- **I am Tenacious** - Let us then with confidence draw near to the throne of grace, that we may receive mercy and find grace to help in time of need. Hebrews 4:16 ESV
- **I am a Comforter** - Blessed be the God and Father of our Lord Jesus Christ, the Father of mercies and God of all comfort, who comforts us in all our affliction, so that we may be able to comfort those who are in any affliction, with the comfort with which we ourselves are comforted by God. 2 Corinthians 1:3-4 ESV
- **I am Mindful** - And do not be conformed to this world, but be transformed by the renewing of your mind, that you may prove what is that good and acceptable and perfect will of God. Romans 12:2 NKJV
- **I am a Helper** - Two are better than one, because they have a good reward for their toil. For if they fall, one will lift up his fellow. But woe to him who is alone when he falls and has not another to lift him up! Ecclesiastes 4:9-10 ESV
- **I am Capable** - I can do all things through Christ who strengthens me. Philippians 4:13 NKJV
- **I am Decisive** - But let your 'Yes' be 'Yes,' and your 'No,' 'No.' For whatever is more than these is from the evil one. Matthew 5:37 NKJV
- **I am a Sharpener** - Iron sharpens iron, and one man sharpens another. Proverbs 27:17 ESV
- **I am Kind** - So then, as we have opportunity, let us do good to everyone, and especially to those who are of the household of faith. Galatians 6:10 ESV

The Tree of Love, LLC
Sharing Who God Says You Are

- **I am Adaptable** - Not that I speak in regard to need, for I have learned in whatever state I am, to be content. Philippians 4:11 NKJV
- **I am an Encourager** - Therefore encourage one another and build one another up, just as you are doing. 1 Thessalonians 5:11 ESV
- **I am Listening** - Consequently, faith comes from hearing the message, and the message is heard through the word about Christ. Romans 10:17 NIV
- **I am a Seeker** - But from there you will seek the Lord your God, and you will find Him if you seek Him with all your heart and with all your soul. Deuteronomy 4:29 NKJV
- **I am a Critical Thinker** - But test everything that is said. Hold on to what is good. 1 Thessalonians 5:21 NLT
- **I am Wise** - "I thank You and praise You, O God of my fathers; You have given me wisdom and might, and have now made known to me what we asked of You, for You have made known to us the king's demand." Daniel 2:23 NKJV
- **I am Competent** - That the man of God may be competent, equipped for every good work. 2 Timothy 3:17 ESV
- **I am Giving** - Give, and it will be given to you. Good measure, pressed down, shaken together, running over, will be put into your lap. For with the measure you use it will be measured back to you. Luke 6:38 ESV
- **I am Educated** - As for you, the anointing you received from him remains in you, and you do not need anyone to teach you. But as his anointing teaches you about all things and as that anointing is real, not counterfeit—just as it has taught you, remain in him. 1 John 2:27 NIV
- **I am Empowered** - And we know that the Son of God has come, and he has given us understanding so that we can know the true God. And now we live in fellowship with the true God because we live in fellowship with his Son, Jesus Christ. He is the only true God, and he is eternal life. 1 John 5:20 NLT

The Tree of Love, LLC
Sharing Who God Says You Are

- **I am Diligent** - The soul of the sluggard craves and gets nothing, while the soul of the diligent is richly supplied. Proverbs 13:4 ESV
- **I am Encouraging Others** - And let us consider how to stir up one another to love and good works, not neglecting to meet together, as is the habit of some, but encouraging one another, and all the more as you see the Day drawing near. Hebrews 10:24-25 ESV
- **I am Respectful** - Don't forget to show hospitality to strangers, for some who have done this have entertained angels without realizing it! Hebrews 13:2 NLT
- **I am a Leader** - Let love be genuine. Abhor what is evil; hold fast to what is good. Love one another with brotherly affection. Outdo one another in showing honor. Do not be slothful in zeal, be fervent in spirit, serve the Lord. Rejoice in hope, be patient in tribulation, be constant in prayer. Contribute to the needs of the saints and seek to show hospitality. Romans 12:9-13 ESV
- **I am Enthusiastic** - Always work enthusiastically for the Lord, for you know that nothing you do for the Lord is ever useless. 1 Corinthians 15:58b NLT
- **I am Able** - Don't be afraid, for I am with you. Don't be discouraged, for I am your God. I will strengthen you and help you. I will hold you up with my victorious right hand. Isaiah 41:10 NLT
- **I am Focused** - Redeeming the time, because the days are evil. Ephesians 5:16 NKJV
- **I am Thoughtful** - He has showered his kindness on us, along with all wisdom and understanding. Ephesians 1:8 NLT
- **I am Compassionate** - You must be compassionate, just as your Father is compassionate. Luke 6:36 NLT
- **I am Bold** - The wicked run away when no one is chasing them, but the godly are as bold as lions. Proverbs 28:1 NLT

The Tree of Love, LLC
Sharing Who God Says You Are

- **I am Knowledgeable** - Asking God, the glorious Father of our Lord Jesus Christ, to give you spiritual wisdom and insight so that you might grow in your knowledge of God. Ephesians 1:17 NLT
- **I am a Learner** - I will instruct you and teach you in the way you should go; I will counsel you with my loving eye on you. Psalm 32:8 NIV
- **I am Confident** - Therefore do not cast away your confidence, which has great reward. Hebrews 10:35 NKJV
- **I am Qualified** - And giving joyful thanks to the Father, who has qualified you to share in the inheritance of his holy people in the kingdom of light. Colossians 1:12 NIV
- **I am Valuable** - Look at the birds. They don't plant or harvest or store food in barns, for your heavenly Father feeds them. And aren't you far more valuable to him than they are? Matthew 6:26 NLT
- **I am Productive** - Yes, I am the vine; you are the branches. Those who remain in me, and I in them, will produce much fruit. For apart from me you can do nothing. John 15:5 NLT
- **I am Resilient** - Do not gloat over me, my enemies! For though I fall, I will rise again. Though I sit in darkness, the Lord will be my light. Micah 7:8 NLT
- **I am Serving Others** - Their responsibility is to equip God's people to do his work and build up the church, the body of Christ. Ephesians 4:12 NLT
- **I am Trying** - Not that I have already obtained all this, or have already arrived at my goal, but I press on to take hold of that for which Christ Jesus took hold of me. Philippians 3:12 NIV
- **I am Unstoppable** - . . . for though the righteous fall seven times, they rise again, but the wicked stumble when calamity strikes. Proverbs 24:16 NIV

Thank you for your purchase! If you are happy with your coloring book, please take a minute and leave us a review on Amazon.

We would love to connect with you via social media:

 @TheTreeOfLoveStore    @thetreeof.love

 @WhoGodSaysIAm    @thetreeoflove

 https://bit.ly/TheTreeofLove-YouTube

The Tree of Love, LLC
Sharing Who God Says You Are

Check Out Our Other Coloring Books

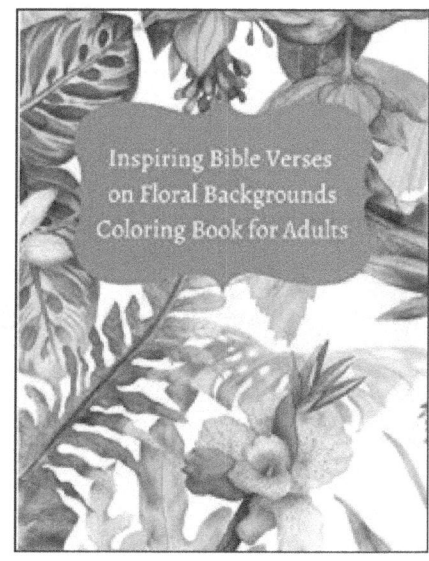

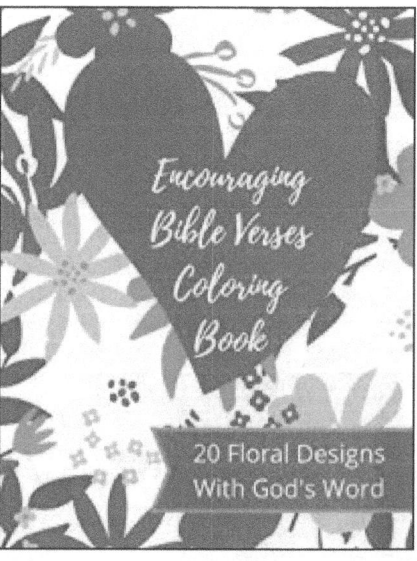

The Tree of Love, LLC
Sharing Who God Says You Are

THE TREE OF LOVE'S MISSION

To put a shirt on 1-million people
"Sociologists tell us that even the most introverted person will influence 10,000 people in his or her lifetime." ~ John Maxwell

1 T-Shirt = 10,000 Influenced

For every t-shirt purchased, The Tree of Love LLC, will donate $1 to *The Gideons International,*
www.Gideons.org

Shop Our Online Store: https://thetreeoflove.org/

Made in United States
Cleveland, OH
17 May 2025

16977924R00052